AMERICAN QUILTER'S SOCIETY

CATALOGUE of SHOW QUILTS

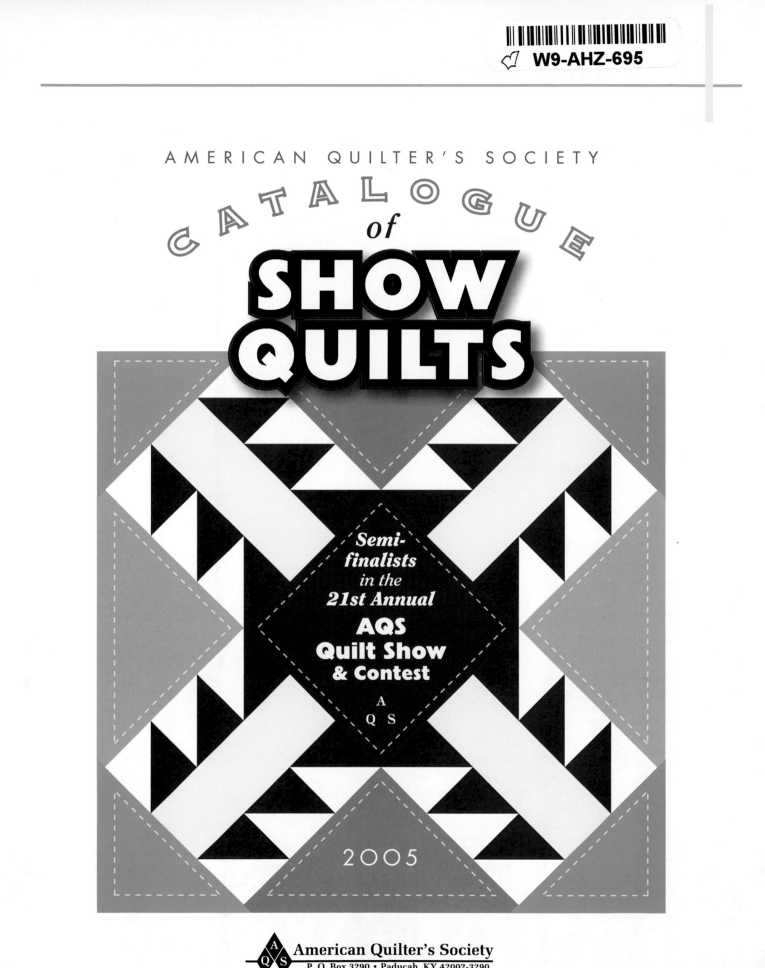

Semi-finalists in the 21st Annual **AQS Quilt Show & Contest**

A Q S

2005

American Quilter's Society
P. O. Box 3290 • Paducah, KY 42002-3290
www.AmericanQuilter.com

Located in Paducah, Kentucky, the American Quilter's Society (AQS) is dedicated to promoting the accomplishments of today's quilters. Through its publications and events, AQS strives to honor today's quiltmakers and their work and to inspire future creativity and innovation in quiltmaking.

EDITOR: BONNIE K. BROWNING
GRAPHIC DESIGN: ELAINE WILSON
COVER DESIGN: MICHAEL BUCKINGHAM
PHOTOGRAPHY: SUPPLIED BY THE INDIVIDUAL QUILTMAKERS

Additional copies of this book may be ordered from the American Quilter's Society, PO Box 3290, Paducah, KY 42002-3290; 800-626-5420 (orders only please); or online at www.AmericanQuilter.com. For all other inquiries, call 270-898-7903.

As the American Quilter's Society begins its twenty-first year, quiltmakers continue to revive time-honored traditional designs, as well as stretch to new heights by exploring new techniques, new materials, and new technologies.

Technology continues to change as more software for designing is developed, computerized sewing machines with stitch regulators are manufactured, and advancements appear in other tools of the trade.

All of these new products give us time to stitch more quilts. Entries came from 46 U.S. states and 12 other countries, exceeding the number of quilts entered in last year's contest.

Plan now to complete your next quilt in time to enter the 2006 AQS Quilt Contest.

Meredith Schroeder

Meredith Schroeder
AQS President and Founder

101, PINK LANAI O KOLOMONA

96" x 96", Lisa Louise Adams, Volcano, HI

Bedquilt - 3rd - applique

102, POPPY GARDEN, 77" x 87"

Linda Benzel, Carlotta, CA

103, BLUEBONNETS AND BUD-DIES

85" x 109", Dorothy Bliss, Brick, NJ

Judges Recognition - 2nd

104, YIN + YANG^2, 66" x 80"

Christine Brasacchio, Bayport, NY

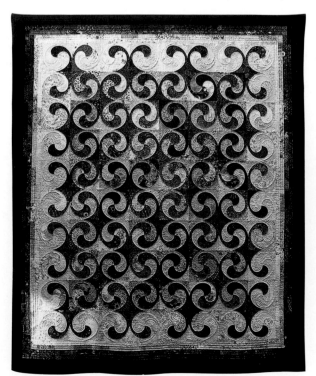

Best of Show

105, BIRDS 'N' ROSES, 83" x 82"

Margaret Docherty, Broompark, Durham, England, UK

106, PRECIOUS FLOWER, ILLIMA, 87" x 111"

Masako Kanda, Nakahara, Kawasaki, Japan

107, TESSIE'S GARDEN OF POSIES

75" x 75", Valerie Martinson, Poulsbo, WA

108, A PRESENT OF ROSES, 77" x 84"

Keiko Miyauchi, Nagano, Japan

Bed quilt - 2nd - applique

Posey Block workshop with Beverly Dunivent

Thru Grandmother's Window, Piece O' Cake Designs

109, **TEACHER'S TREAT: WHITE CHOCOLATE & RASPBERRY SUNDAE**
88" x 88", Ruth E. Ohol, Lockport, NY

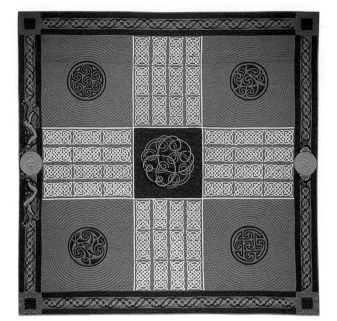

110, **CELTIC SUN MYTH,** 104" x 104"
Donna Olson, Rogersville, MO

111, **RADIANT ROSES,** 90" x 89"
Barbara A. Perrin, Pullman, MI

112, **TWO FOND HEARTS UNITE**
82" x 82", Lahala Phelps, Bonney Lake, WA

Chesapeake Rose, Quilts from the Smithsonian by Mimi Dietrich, Martingale & Company/That Patchwork Place, 1995

Treasures from the Past by Pat Andreatta; Red and Green: An Appliqué Tradition by Jeana Kimball, Martingale & Company/That Patchwork Place, 1990; Album of Memories by Robert Callaham, McCall's Quilting, December 2001

Beel-19t -applique

113, SUBTLE SIXTIES © 2004
81" x 81", LINDA M. ROY, KNOXVILLE, TN

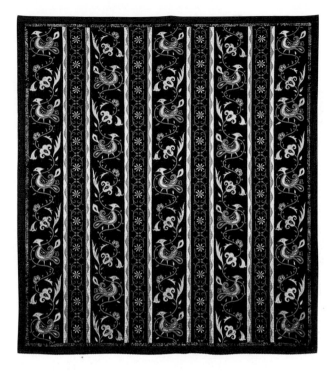

114, VIOLET POEM, 81" x 90"
CHIEKO SHIBUYA, MATSUSAKA, MIE, JAPAN

115, CHALLENGED BY BALTIMORE
98" x 98", BETTY JO SHIELL, VENICE, FL

116, SURROUNDED BY ROSES
82" x 83", HARUMI TAKYO, YOKOHAMA, JAPAN

201, WINTER GARDEN, 86" x 86"

MAGGIE A. BALL, BAINBRIDGE ISLAND, WA

Mariner's Compass workshop with Judy Mathieson

202, GUIDE MY HUNTER HOME

82" x 84", JOYCE LAWRENCE CAMBRON, BOISE, ID

203, FANCY FEATHERS, 82" x 82"

MARGARET CURLEY, PITTSBURGH, PA

204, GRANDMA'S INSPIRATION

82" x 90", KATHLEEN ERBECK, GREEN BAY, WI

Feathered Star Quilt Blocks I by Marsha McCloskey, Feathered Star Productions, Inc.

205, A BED OF TULIPS, 82" x 94"

DOROTHY WEST FOLSOM, MT. VERNON, IL

206, MARINER'S COMPASS, 103" x 111"

MARY ELLEN GLASSMEYER, TUALATIN, OR

207, POWERFUL NEW YORK, 78" x 80"

CHISATO HARAYAMA, MIE, JAPAN

208, SO MANY CHOICES, 72" x 84"

MARIE KRISKY, PITTSBURGH, PA

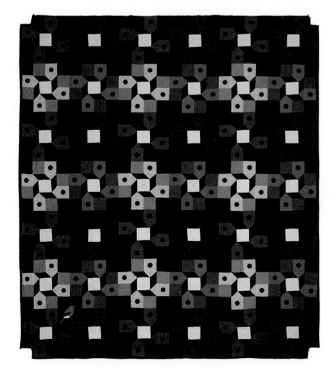

A Quilter's Companion by Dolores A. Hinson, Arco Publishing

Magic Stack-n-Whack® Quilts by Bethany S. Reynolds. American Quilter's Society

209, THE DIVERSION, 70" x 89"
CINDA LANGJAHR, PORT LUDLOW, WA

210, FALL SPLENDOR, 70" x 86"
JUDY L. LAQUIDARA, OWENSBORO, KY

211, THE MAHARAJAH'S GARDEN
81" x 81", JEAN LOHMAR, GALESBURG, IL

212, CASABLANCA, 92" x 92", CLAUDIA CLARK
MYERS & MARILYN BADGER, DULUTH, MN

*Striplate Piecing : Piecing Circle Designs with Speed & Accuracy by Debra Wagner. American Quilter's Society;
Heirloom Machine Quilting: A Comprehensive Guide to Hand-Quilted Effects Using Your Sewing Machine by Harriet
Hargrave. C & T Publishing, Inc. 2004; Mariner's Compass. New Directions by Judy Mathieson. C & T Publishing, Inc.;
Early American Design Motifs by Suzanne E. Chapman. Dover Publications, 2003; background quilting inspired by
Diane Gaudynski*

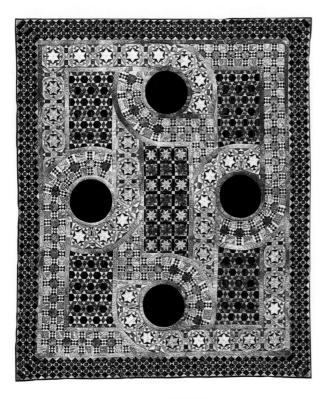

213, A MEMORY OF SICILIA

78" x 94", Tadako Nagasawa, Nagoya, Japan

Bed – 2nd – Pieced

214, MUSCADINE WINE, 90" x 90"

Barbara Newman, Brandon, MS

215, FERN GLADE, 81" x 81"

Hallie H. O'Kelley, Tuscaloosa, AL

216, LOG-CABIN MEDALLION

84" x 84", Fumiko Ohkawa, Kobe, Hyogoken, Japan

Bed – 1st – Pieced

Mocha Java, *Better Homes & Gardens American Patchwork & Quilting Magazine.* Apr 2003

217, GILDED STARS, 78" x 90"

LORETTA PAINTER, NORRIS, TN

218, FARMHOUSE ROAD, 95" x 95"

JUDITH ROBINSON & TINA COLLINS

CAPE GIRARDEAU, MO

Inspired by *The Quilts of Gee's Bend* by John Beardsley, et al., Tinwood Books, 2002

219, JIM'S OCEAN QUILT, 92" x 102"

SUSAN SALSER, PACIFIC PALISADES, CA

220, PLEASE, NO MORE PINKED SAMPLES!

81" x 101", LINDA SCHOLTEN, OXFORD, OH

Santa Fe Sampler workshop with J. Michelle Watts

221, JEMEZ MEMORIES, 92" x 100"

ALEXIS C. SWOBODA, ROSWELL, NM

222, THE SQUARE, 68" x 81"

FUMIE TANAKA, CHIGASAKI, KANAGAWA, JAPAN

223, SALINDA'S GARDEN, 81" x 82"

RENEE THOMPSON, MUKWONAGO, WI

224, REBEL YELL! 84" x 105"

RENÉ WILLIAMS, NORTHRIDGE, CA

Bed - 3rd - Pieced

Nearly Insane by Liz Lois, Liz & Lois Publications

Confederate Courtship, Log Cabin Fever: Innovative Designs for Traditional Quilts by Evelyn Sloppy, Martingale & Company/That Patchwork Place, 2002

Nearly Insane by Liz Lois, Liz & Lois Publications

Quilts, Shelburne Museum: A Book of Postcards. Courtesy Shelburne Museum, Shelburne, Vermont.

225, PIECES OF LIFE, 5,684 OF THEM
96" x 96", ROSEMARY YOUNGS & TAMMY FINKLER, WALKER, MI

301, FOREST WALK, 97" x 81"
CONNIE AYERS, BREMERTON, WA

302, NAUTICAL TREASURE
97" x 97", BARBARA CLEM, ROCKFORD, IL

303, OPTICAL BOXES, 80" x 88"
DIXIE H. HAYWOOD, PENSACOLA, FL

New York Beauty by Karen K. Stone, Dallas, TX

Primrose Lane by Elaine Waldschmitt, The Quilted Closet

Vogue Quilt Juki workshop by Suzuko Koseki

304, BORN TO BE WILD

76" x 96", Susan Liimatta Horn, Sea Cliff, NY

305, PRIMROSE LANE, 74" x 88"

Helen Jacobson, Maxwell, IA

306, PROMISE, 76" x 84"

Noriko Kido, Nagoya, Aichi, Japan

Mixed Techniques - 1st

307, HAPPY FLOWERS, 70" x 90"

Hideko Kubota, Yokohama, Kanagawa, Japan

1800's quilt by Anne Brereton. Quilts of the British Isles by Janet Rae & David Cripps. Deirdre McDonald Books; 1800's quilt in For Purpose & Pleasure: Quilting Together in Nineteenth-Century America by Sandi Fox. Rutledge Hill Press

Memory Bouquet Quilt. The Kansas City Star. Vol. QP1, by Harold & DorothyMae Groves.

308, TURKISH TILES, 91" x 91"

KIM McLean, ROSEVILLE, NSW, AUSTRALIA

309, MEMORY BOUQUET REVISITED

84" x 95", KATHY MUNKELWITZ, ISLE, MN

310, BLOWIN' IN THE WIND, 71" x 81"

MASAE OBARA, TOKOROZAWA, SAITAMA, JAPAN

311, COMPASS IN A LOVE RING

89" x 89", PAULA PETERSON PLATTER, MEAD, OK

Artful Album Quilts: Applique Inspirations from Traditional Blocks by Jane Townswick. Martingale & Company/That Patchwork Place, 2001

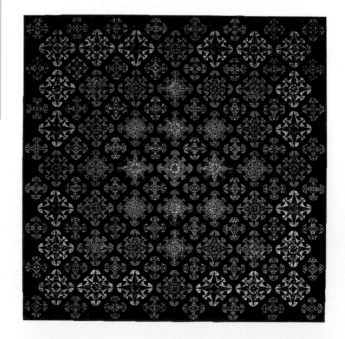

312, BREEZE OVER THE ROOFS, 69" x 80"

Junko Sawada, Yokohama, Kanagawa, Japan

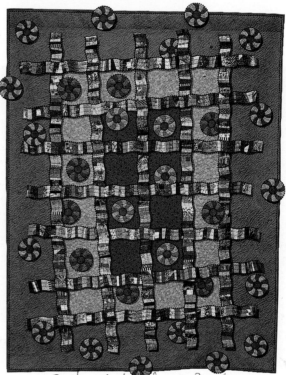

3rd - Mixed Techniques

313, HOPSCOTCH IN ZERO GRAVITY

66" x 86", Valli Schiller, Naperville, IL

314, AUTUMN BREEZE, 82" x 83"

Mildred Sorrells, Macomb, IL

315, A FEW COMPASSES BETWEEN FRIENDS, 91" x 91", Gerry Sweem, Reseda, CA

North Carolina Star, *50 Fabulous Paper-Pieced Stars* by Carol Doak. Martingale & Company/That Patchwork Place, 2000

A Few Compasses Between Friends, *Quilter's® Newsletter Magazine*, #357, Nov. 2003 and #358, Dec. 2003

2nd – Mixed Techniques

316, DAD'S LONE STAR, 93" x 93"

RICKY TIMS, LA VETA, CO

317, A FAMILY CHRISTMAS, 90" x 90"

ANJA TOWNROW, WALSALL, ENGLAND, UK

401, AZAYAKANA: DE AI, 62" x 80"

MIEKO ARAI, IZUMIZAKI, FUKUSIMA, JAPAN

402, ASHLEY'S GARDEN, 106" x 90"

DIANA L. ARCHAMBAULT, PLATTSBURGH, NY

Colorwash Garden Series pattern by Rose Hahn

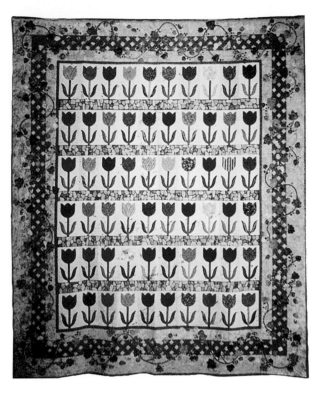

403, MOONLIGHT SONATA, 66" x 90"
MARY ARNOLD, VANCOUVER, WA

404, TIPTOEING THRU THE TULIPS
77" x 91", LINDA BENZEL, CARLOTTA, CA

**405, SEVEN PETALLED SQUASH
BLOSSOM,** 94" x 94", AMY BRIGHT, TUCSON, AZ

406, COMPANY'S COMING, 63" x 104"
CAROLYN CARTER, ADDISON, TX

407, **GROOM'S QUILT,** 85" x 95"
Yvonne Cook, Grants Pass, OR

408, **PRALINE PARFAIT,** 80" x 90",
Martha Cox & Barbara Huthmacher
Ridgecrest, CA

409, **FLIGHT TO FREEDOM,** 85" x 110
Cheryl J. Doody, Alexander, NY

410, **FOREVER,** 90" x 102"
Terry Dowd, Stoughton, MA

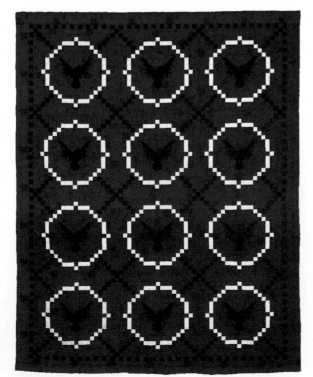

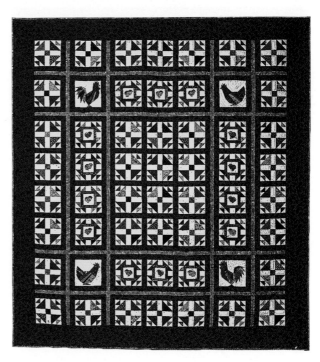

411, LITTLE BROWN BIRD, 92" x 92"

MARY JO EDMISTON, CHOUDRANT, LA

412, RHODE ISLAND REDS, 83" x 92"

DOROTHY WEST FOLSOM, MT. VERNON, IL

413, STAR SYMPHONY, 75" x 96"

KUMIKO FUNAKI, SAITAMA CITY, SAITAMA, JAPAN

1st Entry - 2nd place

414, STARBURST, 107" x 107"

NIKKI GILTNER & DINAH MILLER, PLAINFIELD, IN

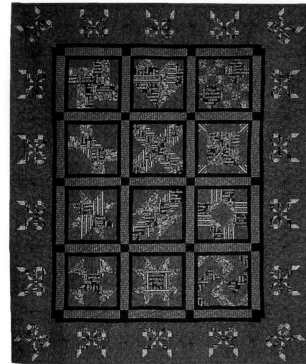

Sweet Lullabies, *Better Homes & Gardens American Patchwork & Quilting, Issue 51,* 2001

Latte Quilt by Kerrie Hay, Quilters' Resource Inc., 2002

415, HOFFMAN CHRISTMAS SAMPLER
71" x 87", DEBORAH GOLDBERG, ALAMOGORDO, NM

416, THE LATTE QUILT, 88" x 88"
FRIEDA GRISCHKOWSKY, STILLWATER, OK

417, FLORAL TREASURE, 93" x 93"
NORMA JONES GRISSOM, CORINTH, MS

418, WATERLILY WALTZ, 96" x 124"
LYNNE HALKETT, PITTSFORD, NY

Sweet Lullabies, *Better Homes & Gardens American Patchwork & Quilting Magazine,* August, 2001

Water Lily motif from *La Plante et ses Applications Ornamentales* by Eugene Grasset (1845-1917)

419, REMEMBERING HIBISCUS

83" x 85", Yumiko Hosono, Shinjuku, Tokyo, Japan

420, KOKORO, 86" x 86"

Atsuko Kuwada, Kawasaki, Kanagawa, Japan

421, FANTASY, 86" x 86", Sandie Lush,
Winterbourne, Bristol, UK

1st Entry - 1st place

422, A SUNBONNET FOR BONNIE

86" x 102", Jimmie Ann McLean, Kalispell, MT

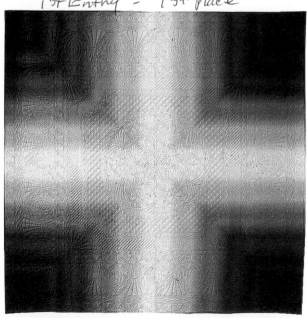

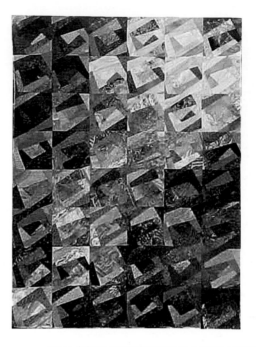

423, CRESSIDA, 96" x 96", Janet Mednick & Deb Karasik, San Francisco, CA

424, THE VIEW FROM MY PORCH 41" x 55", Karen Mihalek, Richfield Township, OH

425, DOTTY PINEAPPLES, 72" x 87" Diane Mooradian, Woodland Hills, CA

426, ALASKA STARS, 108" x 108" Lisa Moore, Sitka, AK

Log Cabin Pineapples workshop with Freddy Moran

427, FRESH SPRING GREEN, 76" x 76"
KEIKO ONANA, ICHIKAWA, CHIBA, JAPAN

428, KAHULUI BREAKWATER, 82" x 84"
CHUNG PRING, BAINBRIDGE ISLAND, WA

429, WEDDING DREAM, 84" x 90"
MASUMI SATO, IKUNO, OSAKA, JAPAN

**430, MEMORIAL OF MY
SEVENTEENTH YEAR,** 82" x 82"
MANAMI SHIMANO, TATEBAYASHI, GUMMA, JAPAN

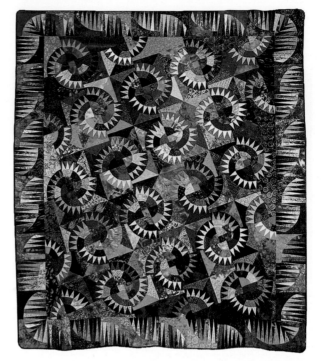

Adapted from EIGHT RED BIRDS quilt by Lorene Liberty Curtis: Lone Star Beauty workshop with Donna Lanman

Montana Cartwheel, Quilt Gallery, Kalispell, MT

431, SOUTHWESTERN STAR, 95" x 95"
KATHRYN SIMS, ALEXIS, IL

**432, DREAMCATCHERS –
A NEW BEGINNING,** 87" x 102"
V. WAYNE SNEATH, NORTHFIELD, IL

433, DOUBLE FLYING GEESE, 84" x 85"
VIOLET SOMMERFELD, HERON, MT

434, 94 YARDS OF LACE, 76" x 76"
SUSAN STEWART, PITTSBURG, KS

1st Entry – 3rd Place

American Quilt Classics from the Collection of Patricia Cox with Maggi McCormick Gordon. Martingale & Company/That Patchwork Place, 2001

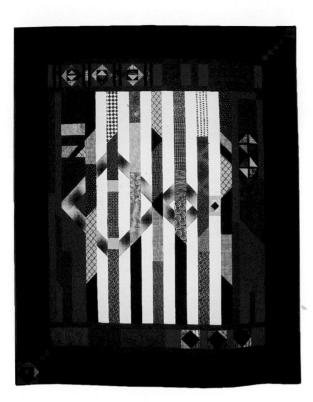

435, DRAWN INSPIRATION, 74" x 94"
PANDORA SYDNOR, ST. CHARLES, MO

Album of Memories by Robert Callaham, McCall's Quilting, Apr. 2001

436, LOG CABIN MEDALLION
80" x 80", MERRILEE TIECHE, NIXA, MO

437, STARDUST MEMORIES, 99" x 99"
RENÉ WILLIAMS, NORTHRIDGE, CA

438, THE SEASONS, 89" x 89"
JOAN WISNIONSKI, LEMONT, IL

Magic Stack-n-Whack by Bethany S. Reynolds, AQS: Rotary Cutting Companion for Feathered Star Quilts by Marsha McCloskey, Feathered Star Productions, Inc.

501, DOUBLE WEDDING QUILT, 96" x 96"
DEBRA BALLARD, MARY JO KERLIN, ELSIE VREDENBURG, MIDLAND, MI

502, CELESTIAL CELEBRATION, 88" x 88"
CLARK COUNTY QUILTERS, WASHOUGAL, WA

503, HEIRLOOM APPLIQUÉ, 70" x 84"
JOANNE DONAHUE & THE PONY EXPRESS QUILTERS, EVANSVILLE, IN

504, THERE ARE STARS IN GRANDMA'S GARDEN, 90" x 102", FAITHFUL CIRCLE QUILTERS GUILD OF DOWNERS GROVE, IL

New England Revisited. *McCall's Quilting,* Apr. 2000

505, STARS AND MEMORIES, 110" x 110"
CYNTHIA GARRETT & THE ST. ANTHONY QUILTERS
EVANSVILLE, IN

506, ALASKA SALMON RUN, 59" x 80"
JOYCE HOFFMAN, ET AL., ANCHORAGE, AK

507, WILD GOOSE CHASE, 81" x 102"
KLONDA HOLT, ET AL., KANSAS CITY, MO

**508, HORN OF PLENTY FOR A NEW
CENTURY,** 83" x 80", KATHY DELANEY, ET AL.,
OVERLAND PARK, KANSAS

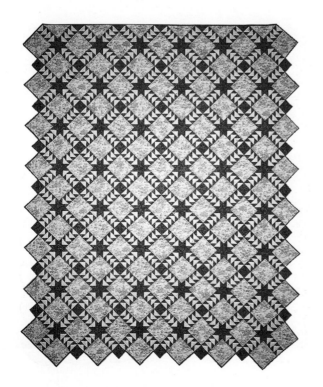

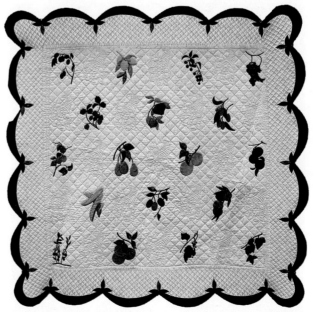

Horn of Plenty for a New Century, The Kansas City Star

Group - 3rd

509, STARS OF THE INLAND SEA, 94" x 94"

CLAUDIA CLARK MYERS AND NORTH COUNTRY QUILTERS
DULUTH, MN

510, BLACK & WHITE JEWELS

80" x 90", MARY QUEDNAU, ET AL., LIBERTYVILLE, IL

511, BEST BUDS, 80" x 96"

VALLI SCHILLER & THE SUGAR LAND BEE, NAPERVILLE, IL

Group - 19+

512, THIRTIES CRAZY SAMPLER

77" x 89", JERRI STROUD, ET AL., WEBSTER GROVES, MO

Group — 2nd

513, GIARDINO DI LUCE, 80" x 81"

MYRL L. TAPUNGOT, ET AL., CAGAYAN DE ORO CITY, MINDANAO, PHILIPPINES

601, DEEP PURPLE, 86" x 89"

SERAR AKAY, ANKARA, TURKEY

514, SPRING IN THE SMOKIES, 72" x 84"

BARBARA WEBSTER, ET AL., BURNSVILLE, NC

602, MY BEAUTY OF MILAN, 79" x 92"

ELEANOR J. CARLSON, CADILLAC, MI

Workshop by Gunsu Gungor, GC Patchwork Studio

603, REJUVENATED CENTENARIANS
77" x 86", Pamela A. Danesi, Brooklyn, NY

604, STARS FROM THE NORTH & THE SOUTH, 72" x 90"
Kelora Lee Goethe, Knoxville, TN

605, IN THE SUNLIGHT, 86" x 86"
Tsueko Kamataki, Chiba City, Chiba, Japan

606, 12 MONTHS OF FLOWER POTS,
86" x 86", Yachiyo Katsuno, Setagaya, Tokyo, Japan

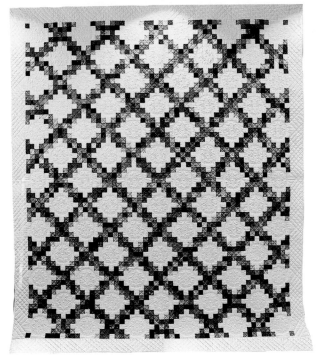

American Chain by Ann Packer, *Quilters' Newsletter Magazine*, Mar. 1990

607, AMERICAN CHAIN, 96" x 110"
IRENE KLEWER, MUNDELEIN, IL

Workshop with Noriko Masui

Handmade — 1st

608, SWEET HEART, 80" x 80"
NORIKO KOBAYASHI, KOUNAN, YOKOHAMA, JAPAN

609, 21ST CENTURY MISSOURI LILY
87" x 87", MARY OWENS, ST. LOUIS, MO

Handmade — 3rd

610, COCO MOON, 82" x 93"
KAZUE SASO, KAMAKURA, KANAGAWA, JAPAN

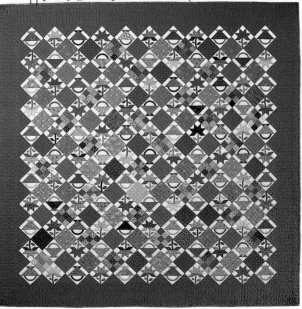

Missouri Folk Art Lily pattern from *The American Quilt Story*, Rodale Press

Workshop with Noriko Masui

611, THE REMEMBRANCE OF DRESDEN
80" x 80", FUSAKO TAKIDO, SHIZUOKA CITY, SHIZUOKA,
JAPAN

612, DREAM IN DREAM, 79" x 89"
FUMIKO TANABE, ICHIHARA, CHIBA, JAPAN

613, ALABASTER RELIEF, 74" x 86"
ZENA THORPE, CHATSWORTH, CA

BestHAND WORKMANSHIP

614, CIRCLE RHAPSODY, 75" x 75"
YUKI YOKOI, KAWAGUCHI, SAITAMA, JAPAN

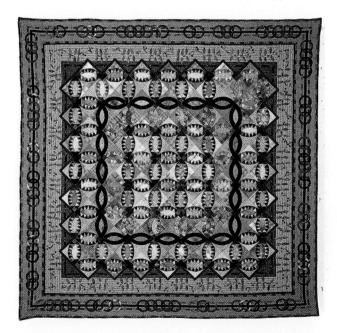

701, BALTIMORE ALBUM, 71" x 71"
JAN M. AMUNDSEN, HORSESHOE BEND, AR

702, PAJAROS BONITOS (BEAUTIFUL BIRDS), 62" x 62", MARY CHOLET RUIZ, TAMPA, FL

703, CELEBRATE THE YEAR OF THE DRAGON, 67" x 66", LETITIA CHUNG
SAN FRANCISCO, CA

704, X-RAY DU SOLEIL (X-RAY OF THE SUN), 68" x 68", SUE GILGEN, MADISON, WI

Large Wall – 2nd – applique

705, BLUE DAISY, 72" x 72"
Saeko Hasumuro, Okayama City, Okayama, Japan

706, ROSE LOVE STORY, 79" x 97"
Michiyo Kato, Tsushima, Aichi, Japan

707, NANI LOKELANI, 101" x 103"
Yachiyo Katsuno, Setagaya, Tokyo, Japan

708, PUFFINS, 78" x 71"
Shirley P. Kelly, Colden, NY

Best— MACHINE WORKMANSHIP

The Best of Baltimore Beauties by Elly Sienkiewicz. C & T Publishing, Inc.

709, THE APPLE ROSES, 73" x 73"
Yoshiko Kitami, Inabe, Mie, Japan

710, PLEASANT DAYS WITH A FLOWER
75" x 75", Yoshiko Koyama, Hidaka, Saitama, Japan

711, CELTIC MYSTERY, 76" x 90"
Lia Laundy, Cornwall, England, UK

712, DON'T WORRY BE HAPPY, 83" x 72"
Cheri Meineke-Johnson, Corinth, TX

Celtic Art: The Methods of Construction by George Bain. Dover Publications

713, BOMBAX TREE, 86" x 94"

MIDORI NAGATANI, GOTENBA, SHIZUOKA, JAPAN

714, NOUVEAU MEANDERING, 72" x 72"

PATRICIA J. SELLINGER, ANN ARBOR, MI

715, THE WILD GARDEN – ECHINACEA

88" x 62", RITA STEFFENSON, URBANA, OH

Large Wall - 1st applique

716, BIRDS IN PARADISE, 78" x 80"

LINDA V. TAYLOR, MELISSA, TX

Best LONG ARM MACHINE Quilting

Serendipity Quilts by Sara Nephew, Clearview Triangle

Large Wall - 3rd applique

717, ARMS OF LOVE, 63" x 77"

RACHEL A. WETZLER, ST. CHARLES, IL

Large Wall - 2nd - Pieced

801, SHIMMERING FOLIAGE, 86" x 86"

FRIEDA L. ANDERSON, ELGIN, IL

802, FLEUR ET FEUILLAGE, 60" x 65"

VIRGINIA ANDERSON, SHORELINE, WA

803, LOOKING HIGH AND LOW

81" x 81", JEAN BIDDICK, TUCSON, AZ

Large Wall - 1st - Pieced

804, LINE DANCING, 64" x 81"
BARBARA CLEM, ROCKFORD, IL

805, STAR SHOWER II, 88" x 88"
BETTE HADDON, DEFUNIAK SPRINGS, FL

806, TRILOGY, 88" x 61"
BARBARA OLIVER HARTMAN, FLOWER MOUND, TX

807, IRRESISTIBLE, 63" x 63"
JANE HELLER, OVERLAND PARK, KS

Maze/Letter T pattern from *Simply Seminole* by Dorothy Hanisko. Quilt Digest Press. 2003;
New York Beauty pattern by Karen K. Stone. Dallas, TX

808, BLACK MAGIC, 85" x 85"
BONNIE LABOWSKY, CHALFONT, PA

809, BUTTERMILK & BLUE, 62" x 63"
DOROTHY LeBOEUF, ROGERS, AR

810, HOT JAVA, 61" x 61"
ALLISON LOCKWOOD, SHELL BEACH, CA

811, PROMETHEAN FLOW, 91" x 67"
MAGGIE MARZIALE, COMMERCIAL POINT, OH

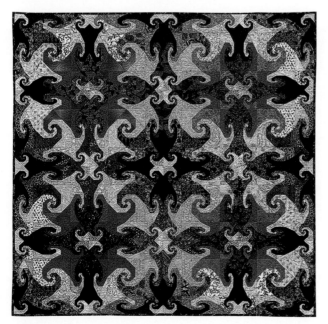

Judy in Arabia. *The Quilt Design Workbook* by Beth & Jeffrey Gutcheon, The Alchemy Press, 1976

812, CELEBRATION, 108" x 108"

Ann Clare Novak, Chino Valley, AZ

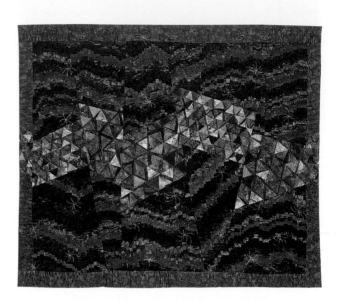

813, FANTASY OF HIGANBANA, 66" x 77"

Hideko Ozawa, Matsumoto, Nagano, Japan

814, RHYTHM OF LIFE, 76" x 76"

Janeen K. Pearson, Ankeny, IA

815, TANGLED WEB, 67" x 67"

Helen Remick, Seattle, WA

Photo by Mark Frey

816, FANTASY STAR, 72" x 72"
JEAN RICHARDSON, LILBURN, GA

817, CRISS-CROSS, 63" x 64"
WENDY SLOTBOOM, SEATTLE, WA

818, TIGER TALES, 94" x 94"
SHIRLEY STUTZ, LORE CITY, OH

819, A PEACEFUL HARMONY (YUUWA)
78" x 78", AKEMI SUGIYAMA, HAMURA, TOKYO, JAPAN

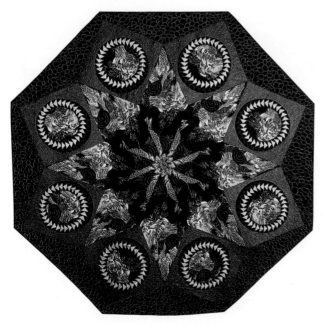

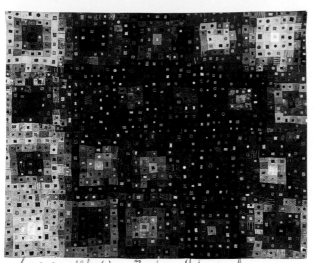

Large Wall - 3rd - Pieced

820, ILLUMINATIONS, 87" x 70"

CAROL TAYLOR, PITTSFORD, NY

821, 24/7, 88" x 88", RACHEL WETZLER

ST. CHARLES, IL

822, FEATHERS IN FLIGHT, 81" x 81"

JULIE WOODS, NORTH EPPING, NSW, AUSTRALIA

901, WE LOVE PEACE, 87" x 74"

TAJIMA AKEMI, HIKI, SAITAMA, JAPAN

NOT AVAILABLE

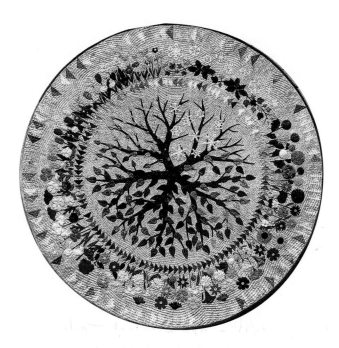

902

903, CIRCLE OF SEASONS, 63" x 63"
KAREN BOGADI, PONCA CITY, OK

904, DELICATE STRENGTH, 80" x 80"
MARY S. BUVIA, GREENWOOD, IN

905, CALIFORNIA AMISH II: FIELDS OF POPPIES, 64" x 64", VALERIE SAUBAN CHAPLA
PLEASANT HILL, CA

Large Wall - 3rd - Mixed Techniques

906, BOUNCIN', 64" x 61"
Susan K. Cleveland, West Concord, MN

Hexagon block by Sara Nephew, Clearview Triangle

907, DIAMONDS IN BLOOM
69" x 75", Joan Dawson, Mill Creek, WA

908, LUSCIOUS VICTORIAN GARDEN
71" x 71", Patricia L. Delaney, Abington, MA

909, LEAVING HOME, 73" x 73"
Barbara Dieges, Tehachapi, CA

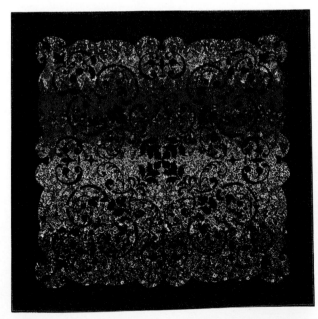

910, **JAPAN BEAUTY (CHERRY BLOSSOM)**
90" x 67", Noriko Endo, Narashino, Chiba, Japan

911, **Z IS FOR ZEBRA,** 102" x 107"
Janet Fogg, Lake Oswego, OR

912, **EVERYDAY BEST,** 72" x 72"
Becky M. Goldsmith, Sherman, TX

913, **THE CLOTH OF AFRICA,** 61" x 77"
Daphne Greig, North Saanich, BC, Canada

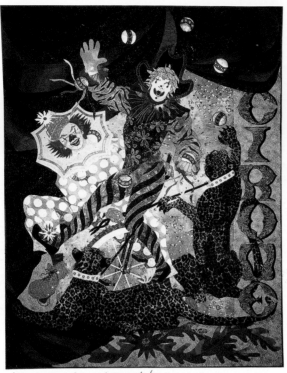

itonorable Mention

914, RINGMASTERS, 60" x 78"
DENISE HAVLAN, PALOS HILLS, IL

916, WOMEN OF THE BIBLE SAMPLER
QUILT, 60" x 102", CAROL HONDERICH, GOSHEN, IN

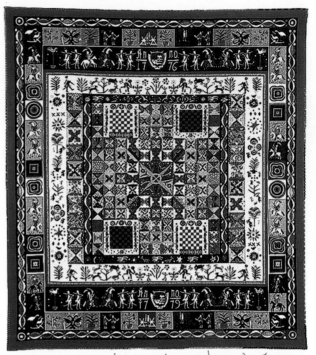

Wall Quilt - 1st ~ Mixed Techniques

915, 1776 – HEARTACHE, HERITAGE AND
HAPPINESS, 98" x 110", PAM HOLLAND, ALDGATE,
SOUTH AUSTRALIA, AUSTRALIA

917, HIDE 'N SEEK, 75" x 75"
JANET KNAPP, FERGUS FALLS, MN

Spring Irish Chain Quilt from *A Bouquet of Quilts: Garden-Inspired Projects for the Home*
by Jennifer Rounds & Cyndy Lyle Rymer, C & T Publishing, Inc.

918, WHEN YOU WISH UPON A STAR!
90" x 90", Yoshiko Koguchi, Mito, Ibaraki, Japan

919, VIOLET STAR GARDEN
80" x 80", Barbara E. Nagengast Lies, Madison, WI

920, TIMES AND SEASONS, 82" x 82"
Susan Magrini, Redding, CA

921, NIGHT BEFORE CHRISTMAS
60" x 68", Kathy McNeil, Marysville, WA

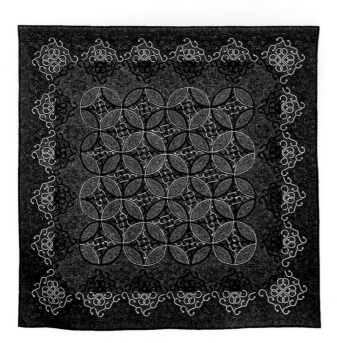

922, SPROUTING OUT, 71" x 71"
Sumiko Minei, Nishitokyo, Tokyo, Japan

923, SAFE HAVEN, 60" x 75", Ellie Neil
Nambucca Heads, New South Wales, Australia

924, MY DEAR MAX, 67" x 77"
Emiko Numasawa, Minato, Tokyo, Japan

925, FOLK ART ROBINS IN LOVE
71" x 71", Pam Pifer, Woodinville, WA

Pattern by Piecemakers Country Store

Designs and Patterns for Embroiderers and Craftspeople: 512 Motifs from the Wm. Briggs and Company Ltd. Album of Transfer Patterns, edited by Marion Nichols, Dover Publications; *Motifs for Crazy Quilting by J. Marsha Michler; Krause Publications; Keepsake Transfer Collection: The Big Book of Over 1000 Designs* by Gerri Sorkin, Better Homes & Gardens

926, ENCHANTED GARDEN, 66" x 66"
ROBERTA RESKUSICH, GLEN CARBON, IL

928, WINDBLOWN ACANTHUS
86" x 94", SHARON SCHAMBER, JENSEN, UT

Appliquéd vase pattern by Sue Nickels, www.sue.nickels.com

927, MEDALLION IN BLOOM, 72" x 72"
JUDY L. ROSS, TRAVERSE CITY, MI

929, AURORA'S GIFT TO THE NORTH
60" x 60", LOUISE SCHOTZ, IRMA, WI

Sidelights, Fanlights and Transoms Stained Glass Pattern Book by Ed Sibbett, Jr.,
Dover Publications

930, SUSTAINED GLASS, 77" x 82"

BARBARA SHIFFLER, STATESBORO, GA

Photograph by Rita Steffenson

931, TRAILING BOUGAINVILLEA

82" x 62", RITA STEFFENSON, URBANA, OH

932, DREAM SPIRITS IN THE NIGHT

63" x 67", AKIKO SUZUKI, HIGASHIOSAKA, OSAKA, JAPAN

933, REFRESHMENT, 77" x 77"

HIROKO TAKARADA, KITA, SAPPORO, JAPAN

Wall Quilt ~2nd~ Mixed Tech.

934, MY FATHER'S SAW, 76" x 85"
YUKIKO TANAKA, HITACHINAKA, IBARAKI, JAPAN

Fancy Cutwork workshop with Jo Coon

935, A CUTWORK VALENTINE, 60" x 60"
CHRIS TARICANI, BURLINGTON, CT

936, ELK RIVER, SUMMER, 74" x 74"
DAVID M. TAYLOR, STEAMBOAT SPRINGS, CO

937, FEATHERED TOPAZ, 80" x 81"
LINDA V. TAYLOR, MELISSA, TX

938, STORY OF ATHENS, 76" x 76"

Kyoko Yano, Sayama, Saitama, Japan

Victorian Patterns and Designs in Full Color by G. A. and M. A. Audsley, Dover Publications

1001, MOTHER EARTH, 49" x 49"

Nancy Baker, DeKalb, IL

1002, COURTHOUSE STEPS, 55" x 78"

Debbi Best, Georgetown, TX

1003, EARLY MORNING REFLECTIONS

60" x 41", Norma Buida, Brentwood, TN

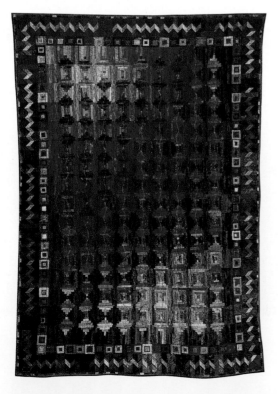

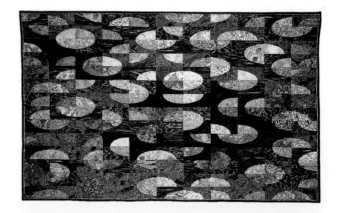

Stars and Rosettes, All Quilt Blocks Are Not Square: Innovative Piecing and Quilting of Hexagons, Triangles, Curves, and More by Debra Wagner, Chilton Book Company, 1995

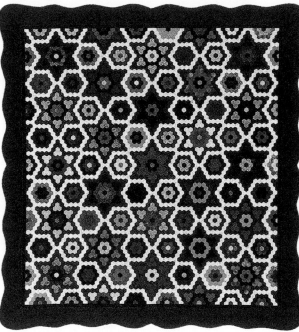

1004, MOSAIC VIRTUES, 57" x 62"

Janet M. Cochran, Fort Collins, CO

Small Wall- 1st -Traditional

1005, PAWS AND REFLECT, 40" x 40"

Sally Collins, Walnut Creek, CA

1006, SOFT BALANCE, 55" x 55"

Judy E. Elwood, Mt. Airy, MD

1007, CIRCLE OF FLOWERS, 58" x 58"

Shoko Ferguson, Clinton, MD

Papercuts and Plenty by Elly Sienkiewicz, C & T Publishing, Inc.

Paper Piecing workshop and pattern by Carol Doak

Small Wall - 3rd - Traditional

1008, FLOWERS FOR MATTI, 53" x 53"
SUSAN LIIMATTA HORN, SEA CLIFF, NY

1010, SNOW BLOSSOMS, 57" x 57"
JANICE MADDOX, ASHEVILLE, NC

Curved Piecing workshop with Jean Dunn

1009, TWIGS, 40" x 48"
ROSEMARY HOUSER, PACIFIC GROVE, CA

1011, A-TISKET, A-TASKET
43" x 43", ALICE MEANS, BOLTON, CT

Baltimore Bouquets by Mimi Dietrich, Martingale & Company/That Patchwork Place, 1992: *Baltimore Tribute Baskets* by Mary Sorensen, Mary Sorensen Design Source

Nature's Garden by Rosemary Makhan, Quilts By Rosemary

Floral Arrangement Appliqué basket pattern by Curiosity, www.curiositypatterns.com

Small Wall - 2nd - Traditional

1012, NATURE'S GARDEN, 54" x 54"

Dorinda Middleton, East Troy, WI

1013, FLOWERS FOR YOU, 58" x 62"

Lieska Motschenbacher and Carolyn Susac,
Colchester, CT

1014, SIZZLING CRYSTALS, 48" x 48"

Susan Nelson, Prior Lake, MN

1015, AUTUMN MANDALA, 58" x 58"

Ann L. Petersen, Aurora, CO

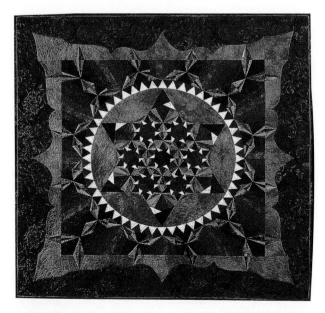

Summer Salsa pattern from *Lone Star Quilts & Beyond: Step-by-Step Projects and Inspiration* by Jan Krentz, C & T Publishing, Inc.

Serendipity Quilts by Sara Nephew, Clearview Triangle

1016, OCTOBER COUNTRY, 59" x 64"

PAM PIFER, WOODINVILLE, WA

1017, PENNY'S BIRD BROOCH

50" x 50", MARINA ROSARIO, APTOS, CA

1018, DOUBLEDEES, 58" x 59"

TESS THORSBERG, MACON, GA

1019, SPRING FLING, 45" x 54"

SUE TURNQUIST, KALAMAZOO, MI

Op-Art Fast, Fun, Fabulous Illusions Quilt Book by Marilyn Doheny, Doheny Publications

The Grammar of Ornament: All 100 Color Plates from the Folio Edition of the Great Victorian Sourcebook of Historic Design by Owen Jones, Dover Publications

37 Sweet Santa Appliques, K. P. Kids & Co.

1020, NOT QUITE AMISH, NOT QUITE WHOLECLOTH, 41" x 42", ELSIE VREDENBURG TUSTIN, MI

1021, SIXTEEN SWEET SANTAS 58" x 69", KATHY YORK, AUSTIN, TX

1022, HEAT WAVE, 42" x 42" S. CATHRYN ZELENY, NAPA, CA

1101, LOOKING UP, 56" x 56" FRIEDA L. ANDERSON, ELGIN, IL

1102, JITTER BUGS, 51" x 51"
PATTY ASHWORTH, OAK RIDGE, TN

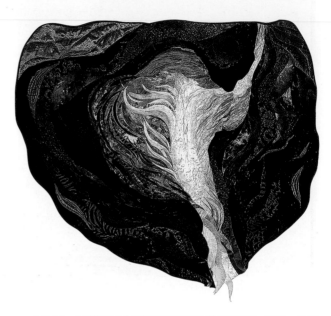

1103, METAMORPHOSIS ROCKS, 57" x 54"
ESTERITA AUSTIN, PORT JEFFERSON STATION, NY

1104, HAPPY TRAILS, 54" x 54"
NANCY BAKER, DeKALB, IL

1105, BLUE RIDGE: ABOVE THE TREE LINE
42" x 41", ARLENE L. BLACKBURN, MILLINGTON, TN

1106, FOREST POND, 40" x 47"
BETH BRADY, MARIETTA, GA

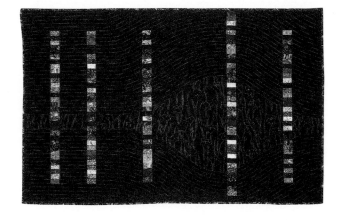

1107, ABSENCE OF COLOR #1
60" x 41", NORMA BUIDA, BRENTWOOD, TN

1108, A ROAD TO HIM, 68" x 52"
EUN RYOUNG CHOI, SEOCHO, SEOUL, KOREA

1109, CROSSROADS, 51" x 51"
SHERRI BAIN DRIVER, CENTENNIAL, CO

1110, AGATE BEACH, 59" x 41"
PAT DURBIN, EUREKA, CA

1112, THE SUNSTITCHERS GO TO PADUCAH, 42" x 52", MARGIE ENGEL
SATELLITE BEACH, FL

Elinor Peace Bailey embroidery card

1111, ELECTRIC FLOWERS – SUMMER
42" x 52", ROBBI JOY EKLOW, THIRD LAKE, IL

1113, GEORGE'S GARDEN, 48" x 53"
ANN FAHL, RACINE, WI

Best
Brother Machine Quiting — Wall quilt

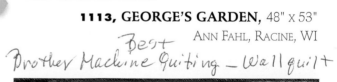

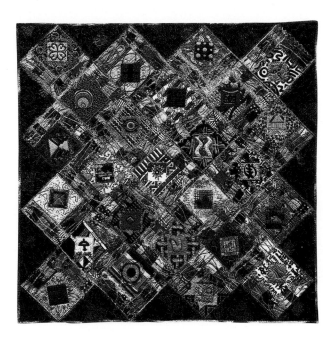

1114, MUMBO-JUMBO, 51" x 51"
CINDY CILLICK GEIST, BRIGHTON, MI

1115, A YOUNG MAN'S FANCY, 40" x 46"
SHERRIE GROB, MURPHYSBORO, IL

1116, WE FIX BROKEN HEARTS
51" x 63", ELLEN GUERRANT, CHARLOTTE, NC

1117, ESSENCE OF PLEASURE, 44" x 55"
JULIE HADDRICK, BLACKWOOD, SOUTH AUSTRALIA
AUSTRALIA

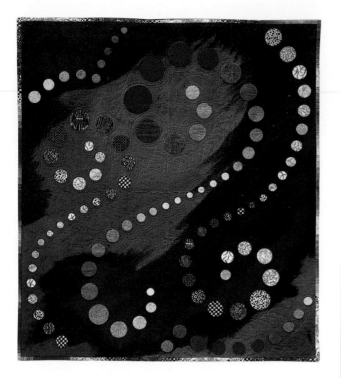

1118, CIRCLES, 43" x 48"
NANCY HAHN, ST. PETERS, MO

1119, THE WHOLE KITTEN KABOODLE
55" x 41", SARADEAN HALLMAN, WEST COLUMBIA, SC

1120, GOING IN CIRCLES II, 46" x 46"
GLORIA HANSEN, HIGHTSTOWN, NJ

1121, HEAT WAVES X: MIRAGE
49" x 42", LYNNE G. HARRILL, JESUP, GA

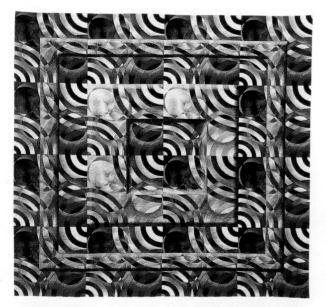

1122, SAFETY FIRST, 53" x 71"

Barbara Oliver Hartman, Flower Mound, TX

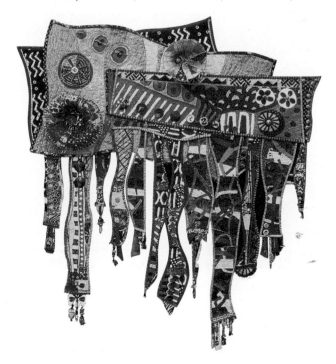

1123, MY WONDERFUL HUSBAND

42" x 48", Tone Haugen-Cogburn, Maryville, TN

1124, BETWEEN DAY AND DREAM

57" x 83", Margarete Heinisch, West Hills, CA

McCall's Hand Quilting – Wall quilt
Best

1125, OUT-OF-CONTROL CURVACEOUS

SHAPES, 54" x 54", Dianne S. Hire, Northport, ME

Eureka pattern by Debbie Bowles, Maple Island Quilts

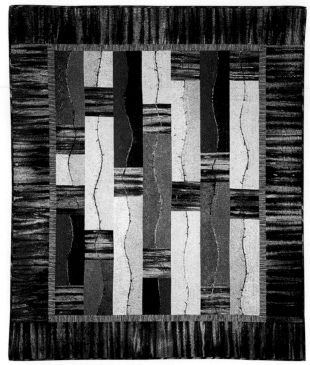

1126, EUREKA, 43" x 52"
KLONDA HOLT, KANSAS CITY, MO

1127, TWO TO TANGO, 40" x 50"
ANN HORTON, REDWOOD VALLEY, CA

1128, A TRIUMPH OF TULIPS
52" x 43", MELODY JOHNSON, CARY, IL

Small Wall - 1st - Non traditional

1129, BLUE MOON HAUTE COUTURE
SERIES, 46" x 69", JANE KENNEDY, LONE JACK, MO

1130, LOVE GROWS, 45" x 45"
KIM KLOCKE, ROCHESTER, MN

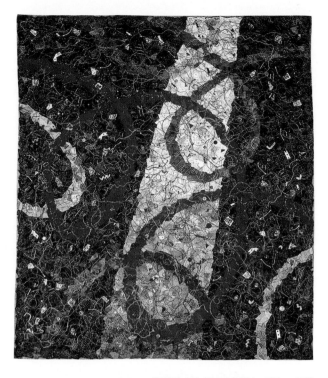

1131, SPIRAL DANCE, 43" x 50"
PAT KROTH, VERONA, WI

1132, GORILLA XING, 40" x 40"
CINDA LANGJAHR, PORT LUDLOW, WA

1133, COMPLEMENTARY WITH AN "E"
50" x 68", KATHLEEN LOOMIS, LOUISVILLE, KY

1134, FIESTA FLORIBUNDA II, 50" x 49"

ANNE LULLIE, LAKE IN THE HILLS, IL

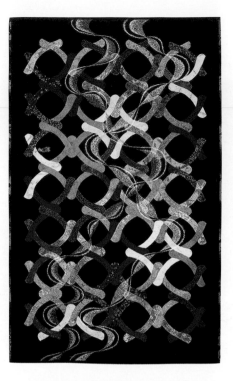

1135, COMPLEX CHORDS, SIMPLE MELODIES, 40" x 65", JANICE MADDOX
ASHEVILLE, NC

1136, THE TABLE IS SET, 54" x 72"

TUULA MÄKINEN, TAMPERE, FINLAND

1137, UNDER THE SUNFLOWERS

42" x 56", BARBARA BARRICK MCKIE, LYME, CT

Small Wall - 3rd - Non-Trad.

1138, FLORAL POLYGON, 57" x 57"
HALLIE H. O'KELLEY & CHARLES O' KELLEY,
TUSCALOOSA, AL

1139, THE BECKONING, 51" x 51"
MARTI PLAGER, LOUISVILLE, KY

1140, PROCESSIONAL CARPET
53" x 64", LESLIE REGO, SUN VALLEY, ID

**1141, FITNESS CLASS AT THE SENIOR
CENTER,** 45" x 72", DEE ROSING, EDGEWOOD, KY

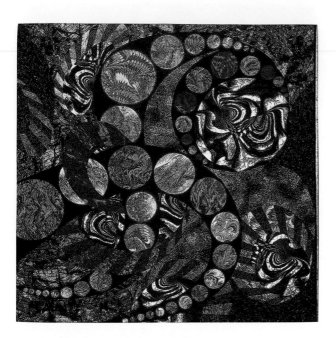

1142, MARBLED MADNESS, 41" x 41"
LUCY SILLIMAN, FORT SCOTT, KS

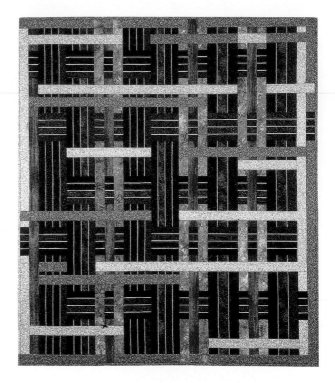

1143, STREET MUSIC, 46" x 54"
WENDY SLOTBOOM, SEATTLE, WA

1144, TROPICAL CANOPY, 59" x 44"
JUDY SMITH-KRESSLEY, WAYNE, PA

1145, VENTURE, 42" x 54"
JANET STEADMAN, CLINTON, WA

Photo © Judy Smith-Kressley

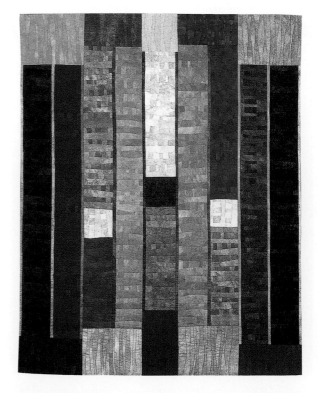

1146, TRANSITIONS, 47" x 98"
CAROL TAYLOR, PITTSFORD, NY

Small Wall - 2nd - Non-Trad.

1147, RHAPSODY IN GREEN, 59" x 60"
RICKY TIMS, LA VETA, CO

1148, ROAMING THE SAVANNA
43" x 51", JOAN DUBAY TULLY, DUBUQUE, IA

1149, OCTOBER WOODS, 42" x 44"
CINDY VOUGH, NICHOLASVILLE, KY

1150, MORNING SKY ABLAZE, 52" x 42"

Beth Frisbie Wallace, Francestown, NH

1151, MOUNTAIN MINT, 50" x 72"

Barbara Webster, Burnsville, NC

1152, SPACESCAPE: WITH ANOTHER VOICE, 59" x 58", S. Cathryn Zeleny, Napa, CA

1201, MATERIAL GIRLS, 55" x 68"

Faye Anderson, Broomfield, CO

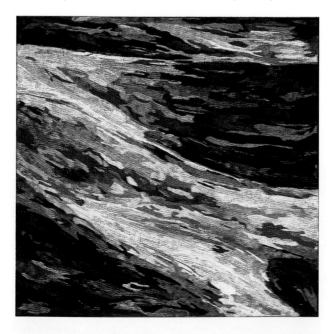

Pictorial – 1st

1202, WANTED, 52" x 46"
NANCY S. BROWN, OAKLAND, CA

1203, NIGHT FISHERMAN, 56" x 65"
ROSELLEN CAROLAN, AUBURN, WA

1204, ELECTRIC FLOWERS NIGHTTIME
42" x 54", ROBBI JOY EKLOW, THIRD LAKE, IL

1205, FLIGHT OF FANCY, 42" x 42"
MARIA ELKINS, DAYTON, OH

1206, VASES WITH TULIPS AND MAGNOLIAS, 45" x 50"
ISABELLE ETIENNE-BUGNOT, SOISY-SUR-SEINE, FRANCE

1207, RED HATS, 49" x 66"
MARILYN FALLERT, SAINT LOUIS, MO

1208, BLUE NUDE, 50" x 40"
MERRY FITZGERALD, DVM, LAKE GROVE, NY

1209, REVELATIONS, 40" x 50"
LAURA FOGG, UKIAH, CA

The Middle Ages by Edmund V. Gillon Jr., Dover Publications; Medieval Costume in England and France by Mary G. Houston, Dover Publications

1210, AUTUMN TRIPTYCH, 54" x 40"
CATHY GEIER, WAUKESHA, WI

1211, WAR OF THE ROSES, 53" x 83"
CAROL GODDU, MISSISAUGA, ONTARIO, CANADA

1212, FIVE FLUFFY FEATHERED FRIENDS
40" x 58", PATRICIA M. GOFFETTE, EDMONDS, WA

1213, JEALOUS OF GINGER, 40" x 50"
VICKY GROOM, WILLITS, CA

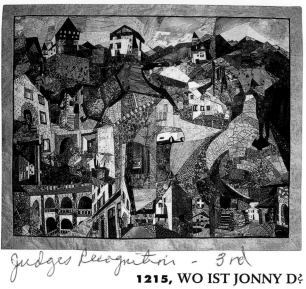

Judges Recognition - 3rd

1215, WO IST JONNY D?
(TOURING SWITZERLAND)
53" x 42", Karen Hanken, Jacksonville, OR

1214, SLICED PINEAPPLE, 55" x 42"
Dianna Grundhauser & Joan Davis, Makawao, HI

1216, SUNSET HILLS, 44" x 50"
Sachiko Hasegawa, Hitachinaka, Ibaraki, Japan

1217, RED BOAT, 49" x 42", Tone Haugen-
Cogburn & Bridget Wilson Matlock, Maryville, TN

Art Glass Pattern #134 by Allen Kenoyer. www.allenkenoyerglass.com

1218, OCEAN-LIFE AT BALI HAI
53" x 78", Jane H. Haworth, Auburn, CA

1220, FOXY SISTERS, 57" x 57"
Ann Horton, Redwood Valley, CA

1219, AURORA SENTINEL, 55" x 48"
Jacqué J. Holmes, Big Bear Lake, CA

1221, DEBKE DANCING IN JERUSALEM
40" x 50", Leila Kazimi, Redwood Valley, CA

1222, MUCHACHAS TEHUANAS
40" x 50", SUSAN G. KERR, UKIAH, CA

1223, FLAMENCO PASSION
40" x 50", BETTY LACY, UKIAH, CA

1224, AT HOME IN IRELAND, 47" x 45"
BERYL LAWSON, HARRISONBURG, VA

1225, DANCING WITH THE DRAGON
40" x 50", DORTHY LEDFORD, TALMAGE, CA

Best Wall Quilt

1226, UNEXPECTED BEAUTY, 51" x 67"
Sandra Leichner, Albany, OR

1227, WHEN MORNING GILDS THE SKIES
43" x 43", Rebecca Muir MacKellar, Canton, NY

1228, EYE-CATCHING EYESPOT, 47" x 47"
Inge Mardal & Steen Hougs, Chantilly, France

1229, PAPILLIO AMARYLLIS
57" x 72", Barbara Barrick McKie, Lyme, CT

1230, SQUAWKER, 47" x 40"
KATHY MCNEIL, MARYSVILLE, WA

1231, 335 NORTH 6TH STREET, PADUCAH
42001, 57" x 47", AYNEX MERCADO, PADUCAH, KY

1232, OCTOBER AFTERNOON
40" x 52", BARBARA MILLER, NORMAL, IL

**1233, ANNA & THE KING BRING
ELEGANCE TO THE POLKA**
40" x 50", JOYCE PATERSON, UKIAH, CA

1234, TUSCAN VILLA, 51" x 43"
RUTH POWERS, CARBONDALE, KS

1235, OVER THE PORCH RAIL
50" x 56", SHARON V. ROTZ, MOSINEE, WI

1236, WATCHING JAKE SKATE WITH THE PUCK... PRICELESS
40" x 53", KARI L. RUEDISALE, LANSING, MI

1237, CASCADE, 41" x 70"
LINDA S. SCHMIDT, DUBLIN, CA

1238, THE EVENT, 50" x 50"
ALEXANDRA SCHWEITZER, CRYSTAL LAKE, IL

1239, RED CANOE, 45" x 41"
NATALIE SEWELL, MADISON, WI

1240, BIJAGOS WARRIOR, 40" x 60"
SARAH ANN SMITH, CAMDEN, ME

1241, THIS LITTLE LIGHT OF MINE
53" x 44", CATHY PILCHER SPERRY, CINCINNATI, OH

"Pilcher Grandkids" painting by Kara Pilcher; used with permission

1242, BEACH GURLY, 46" x 40"
Nancy Sterett, Owensboro, KY

Photo credit: Judy Smith-Kressley

1243, TOUCAN AT TWILIGHT
40" x 48", B. J. Titus, Coatesville, PA

1244, UP FROM THE DEPTHS,
54" x 43", Sue Turnquist, Kalamazoo, MI

1245, BEYOND THE BACK DOOR
40" x 46", Donna J. Van Dyke, Sarasota, FL

Pictorial-3rd

1246, LADY OF THE LAKE, 52" x 79"
ANNA VANDEMARK, BUTTERNUT, WI

1247, GRANDMA ELLA'S SCHOOLHOUSE
44" x 44", PHYLLIS L. WERGES, CANANDAIGUA, NY

1248, ONCE WE WERE YOUNG, 46" x 42"
MARY WILBER WIRCHANSKY, SCHENEVUS, NY

1249, THE CONGREGATION, 53" x 42"
MARLENE BROWN WOODFIELD, LAPORTE, IN

1301, EAGLE – BANNER OF THE FREE

51" x 55", Mindy Beveridge, Troy, MI

1302, EGG MONEY QUILT

52" x 82", Sue Bouchard, Vista, CA

1303, BLACK, WHITE & WILD

57" x 52", Christine Bryden, Mosheim, TN

1st entry – 2nd Place

1304, FIREWORK, 45" x 51"

Cynthia Cannone, Norway, ME

Summer Salsa pattern from Lone Star Quilts & Beyond: Step-by-Step Projects and Inspiration by Jan Krentz, C & T Publishing, Inc.

1305, **RADIATING RAINBOW,** 47" x 47"

ANNE COMER, EAST HADDAM, CT

1306, **INDIAN SUMMER,** 47" x 47"

AMY CUNNINGHAM-WALTZ, WALTHAM, MA

1307, **FOLK ART FANCY,** 60" x 77"

PAMELA DAVIS, EDGEMONT, AR

1308, **WINDSWEPT,** 55" x 55"

NANCY B. DICKEY, MAGNOLIA, TX

Once Upon A Time...In the Country by Sarah Sporrer, Indygo Junction, Inc.

1309, WEBMASTER, 55" x 40"

GRACE J. ERREA, LAGUNA NIGUEL, CA

1310, CAROLINA ON MY MIND

54" x 45", LOU ANN ESTES, PADUCAH, KY

1311, LOOKING UP, 47" x 50"

MELISSA FRANKEL, CULVER CITY, CA

1312, CHAISE LOUNGES, 47" x 48"

JOAN FRANTZ, FT. MYERS, FL

1313, SPIRIT DANCER, 56" x 56"
Lynn Gilles, Presque Isle, WI

1314, LOG CABIN BARN RAISING, 51" x 66"
Nikki Giltner & Dinah Miller, Plainfield, IN

1315, NIWDOOG, 65" x 70"
Cindi Goodwin, Naples, FL

1316, SPIRIT OF NATIVE AMERICANS
52" x 60", Karen L. Guthrie, Marshall, MO

Calico Compass original quilt owned by Anne Olsen, *Quiltmaker*, Sept. 2003

Native American Designs for Quilting by Joyce Mori, American Quilter's Society

1317, SEA TURTLE, 42" x 58"
Jutta Halpin, Glastonbury, CT

**1319, THE ROARING '20S...
THOSE WERE THE DAYS**
41" x 50", Valeta Hensley, Flemington, MO

1318, PEACE AT SUNSET, 40" x 40"
Molly Yao Hamilton, Tehachapi, CA

1320, WALLPAPER ROSES, 42" x 40"
Pat Hiller, Harrison Township, MI

Spanish Dancer. *Vintage Tinted Linens & Quilts* by Brenda Hopkins & Nori Koenig.
Design Originals. www.d-originals.com

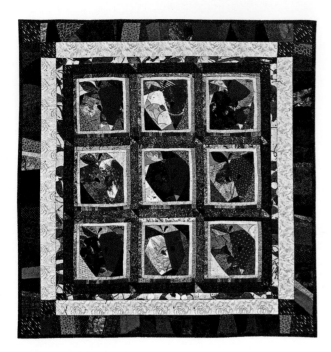

1321, APPLEFEST, 40" x 41"
LOUISE LoPINTO HUTCHISON, WARWICK, NY

1322, SWIM BABY SWIM, 47" x 47"
BECKY JACKSON, CORINTH, TX

1323, 700 WATTS OF SMOOTHIE POWER
47" x 47", AUDREY KAYS, STAUNTON, IL

1324, TEA TIME AND ROSES AT MY CABIN
61" x 42", BECKY KELHER, CAÑON CITY, CO

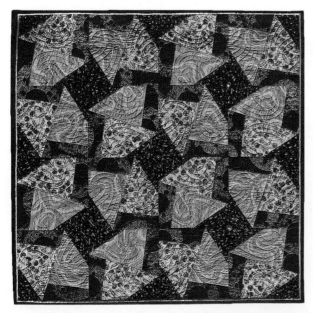

Tea Party by Caroline Reardon, Quilter's® Newsletter Magazine, July/Aug. 1992

1325, SUMMER LAKE AT TREELINE

51" x 42", ANNETTE KENNEDY, LONGMONT, CO

1326, SO MANY FLOWERS, SEW LITTLE TIME, 40" x 45", TERRI KIRCHNER, MEQUON, WI

1327, DIAMOND SQUARE, 43" x 43"

JANET LINDSAY, SAN DIEGO, CA

1328, CELESTIAL CROWNS, 50" x 50"

TOBY LISCHKO, ROBERTSVILLE, MO

1st entry - 1st place

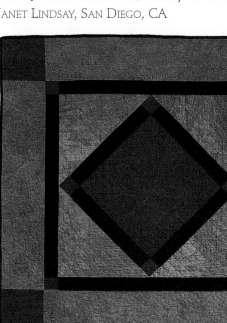

1329, MELLIFLUOUS AFFAIR, 56" x 64"
SUSAN MALLETT, SIOUX FALLS, SD

1330, THE ALLIGATOR FROM THE GREAT NORTHWEST, 50" x 60"
NANCY MILLER, SUMMERVILLE, SC

1331, SUNRISE AT LAKE ADGER
57" x 70", VERONICA MORIARTY, SPARTANBURG, SC

1332, MOMENT, 47" x 54"
MADALENE AXFORD MURPHY, WELLSBORO, PA

Insomnia pattern by Ale Rossmann, Lotusland's

Texas Tease by Dereck C. Lockwood, www.lockwoodquilts.com

1333, INSOMNIA, 43" x 43"

LEORA Y. NEEDHAM, SANDPOINT, ID

1334, MEMORIES OF ENCHANTMENT

56" x 56", JACKIE O'LAUGHLIN, METAMORA, IL

1335, CARRIE HALL SAMPLER, 43" x 43"

LORRAINE OLSEN, SPRINGFIELD, MO

1336, FLORAL FANTASY, 57" x 71"

MARY JOYCE SCHWALBE OVANS, WEBSTER, MN

Carrie Hall Blocks: Over 800 Historical Patterns from the College of the Spencer Museum of Art, University of Kansas by Bettina Havig, American Quilter's Society; The Romance of the Patchwork Quilt in America by Carrie A. Hall and Rose G. Kretsinger, 1935, The Caxton Printers, Ltd., Caldwell, Idaho

Floral Reflections Collection by Binky Brown Takahashi, Quilt Nouveau Designs

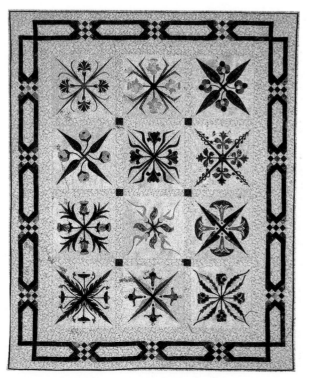

1337, SANTA'S NEIGHBORHOOD
45" x 56", Grace Owen, Prairie Grove, AR

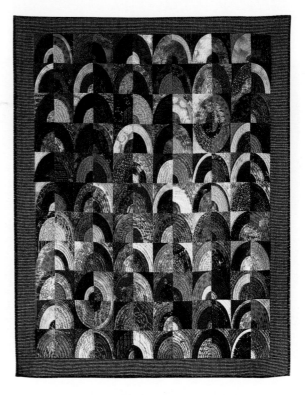

1338, WAVES OF COLOUR, 55" x 72"
Frieda Oxenham, Peeblesshire, Scotland, UK

1339, MOON TANGO, 52" x 72"
Charla K. Pauls, Johnson, KS

1340, ROSEVILLE, 53" x 56"
June Pease, Pfafftown, NC

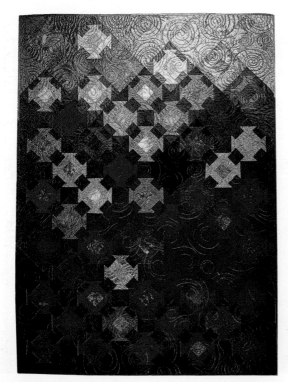

1341, LEGEND OF CHILDHOOD LOST
47" x 44", Paula Tomlin Ridley, Mountain Rest, SC

1343, MOON GLOW, 59" x 59"
Jean Marie Semrow, Milwaukee, WI

1st entry – 3rd place

1342, OMOIDE (MEMORIES)
55" x 55", Vivian Ritter, Evergreen, CO

1344, JOY, 41" x 50"
Brenda Smith, Flagstaff, AZ

Cutting Double Workshop with Sandi Cummings

Embroidery designs from Husqvarna Viking

1345, **HEIRLOOM DREAMS,** 56" x 56"
Susan Stewart, Pittsburg, KS

1346, OCEAN, 45" x 58"
Tracy McCabe Stewart, Grayslake, IL

1347, PETALS OF MY HEART
54" x 48", Linda Stoeffler, Ballwin, MO

1348, FASHIONISTA, 43" x 63"
Debra Svitil, Alpharetta, GA

Petals of my Heart: A Wildflower Collection by McKenna Ryan, Pine Needles

1349, FLOWERING HEARTS FANTASY
55" x 66", PATSY THOMPSON, HOLLAND, OH

1350, ESPAÑA, 50" x 50"
JEANIE SAKRISON VELARDE, CORDOVA, TN

1351, PORTALS: PORTUGAL, 61" x 43"
RUTH VINCENT, SEATTLE, WA

1352, NEW DAWN, 41" x 67"
BARBARA SHAPEL YANO, WASHOUGAL, WA

1401, MYSTERY STARS, 42" x 42"

BONNIE BERGMAN, ET AL., LAKE TOMAHAWK, WI

1402, MOVE OVER COCO, 48" x 74"

FRIDAY MORNING GROUP, COS COB, CT

1403, PIECERS, TALKERS & APPLIQUÉRS

59" x 71", LYNNE G. HARRILL, ET AL., JESUP, GA

1404, OHIO BICENTENNIAL QUILT

1803–2003, 59" x 59"

QUILTING STARS OF OHIO GUILD, CANTON, OH

Group - 2nd

Group - 1st place

1405, GHOST QUILTERS IN THE SKY
52" x 64", ANN SEELY & JOYCE STEWART
TAYLORSVILLE, UT

Group - 3rd

1406, HANDS & HEARTS OF HOSPICE
60" x 78", CATHERINE SIMMONS, ET AL., BOONVILLE, IN

1407, GEORGIE ON MY MIND, 50" x 43"
JULIE WELLS, LESLIE JOHNSON, BECKY COHEN
DENVER, CO

1501, THE TREES, 16" x 16"
SHARON BURRER, SILVERDALE, WA

Hollyhock, *Encyclopedia of Classic Quilt Patterns* by Patricia Wilens, Oxmoor House

1502, PRIMARILY TRADITIONAL, 23" x 23"

KATHLEEN CARLSON, BRIDGETON, MO

1503, LONE STAR, 16" x 16"

SALLY COLLINS, WALNUT CREEK, CA

1504, SHELBURNE REVISITED, 23" x 22"

JUDITH DAY, LINDFIELD, NSW, AUSTRALIA

1505, NAVIGATOR, 16" x 16"

KUMIKO FRYDL, LONDON, UK

Replica of the HORSE AND BIRDS ALBUM QUILT, ca. 1850, from the Shelburne Museum, Shelburne, Vermont

1507, GRANDMOTHER'S IRISH CHAIN
22" x 22", JAYNETTE HUFF, CONWAY, AR

1509, MINIATURE PRIMROSE LANE
18" x 22", HELEN JACOBSON, MAXWELL, IA

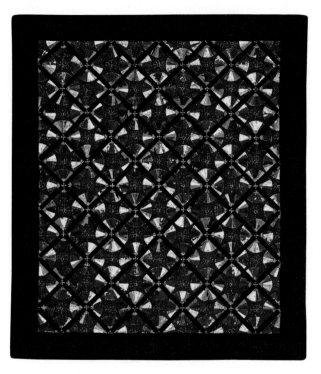

1508, BLACK-EYED SUSAN, 19" x 22"
SUSAN JACKSON, ARROYO GRANDE, CA

1510, LA MOISSON D'OR, 10" x 10"
MARIE KARICKHOFF, SOUTH LYON, MI

Primrose Lane by Elaine Waldschmitt, The Quilted Closet

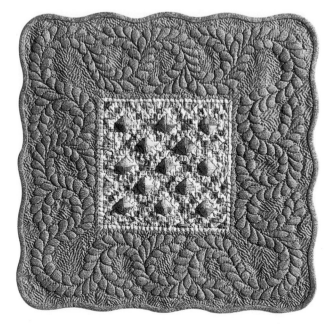

1511, MY FAVORITE ROSES, 21" x 21"
Keiko Kitamura, Nishinomiya, Hyogo, Japan

1512, SAFE HARBOR, 15" x 15"
Pat Kuhns, Lincoln, NE

1513, YELLOWLICIOUS, 18" x 18"
Diane Lane, Wichita, KS
Miniature — 3rd

1514, SHE USED TO LIVE HERE
23" x 21", Margot McDonnell, Phoenix, AZ

Autumn Harvest designed by Bonnie Leman, Mary Leman Austin and Judy Martin. Quiltmaker Magazine. Fall/Winter 1982

1515, MAY TO SEPTEMBER
14" x 17", MARIE MOORE, HOUSTON, TX

1516, BEJEWELLED, 18" x 18", LIUXIN NEWMAN
TURRAMURRA, NSW, AUSTRALIA

1517, LA PETIT II, 23" x 23"
JOANIE ZEIER POOLE, SUN PRAIRIE, WI

1518, MOM, 13" x 17", SUZANNE M. RIGGIO
WAUWATOSA, WI

Quilts: Old and New, A Similar View by Paul D. Pilgrim and Gerald E. Roy. American Quilter's Society

Honorable Mention

1519, WHISPER OF CHAMPAGNE
20" x 20", SHARON SCHAMBER, JENSEN, UT

1520, MY FLOWER GARDEN, 17" x 17"
MIYOKO SHODA, KUMAGAYA, SAITAMA, JAPAN

1521, PINEAPPLE FLAMBÉ, 17" x 19"
JUDY SPIERS, FOXWORTH, MS

Miniature – 2nd

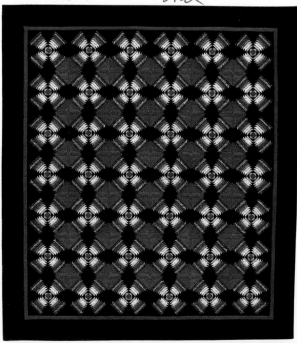

1522, GILDING THE LILY, 11" x 12",
PAT M. STOREY, BRIDGNORTH, SHROPSHIRE, UK

Tucks, Textures & Pleats by Jenny Rayment, J. R. Publications, 1994; Tucks & Textures Two by Jennie Rayment, J. R. Publications, 1997

Photo of antique quilt from the James Collection. *Quilters' Newsletter Magazine*, Issue 305, 1998

1523, ANONYMOUS 1830, 15" x 17"
Loretta C. Sylvester, Palm Coast, FL

1524, SPRING, 19" x 19"
Trudy Søndrol Wasson, Eden Prairie, MN

We are proud to present the sponsors for the 21st annual AQS Quilt Show & Contest. Each category and event has its own sponsor from the world of quilting. To open the show, the company representatives present the cash awards at the Awards Presentation on Tuesday evening.

Best of Show . . . . .Hancock's of Paducah
Hand Workmanship Award . . . . .American Quilter's Society
Machine Workmanship Award . . . . .Bernina® of America, Inc.
Longarm Machine Quilting Award . . . . . . .Gammill Quilting Machine Company
Best Wall Quilt . . . . .RJR Fabrics
Small Wall Hand Workmanship Award . . . .McCall's Quilting
Small Wall Machine Workmanship Award . .Brother® International
Bed Quilts
    Appliqué . . . . .Mountain Mist®
    Pieced . . . . .Hobbs Bonded Fibers
    Mixed Techniques . . . . .EZ Quilting® by Wrights®
    1st Entry in AQS Quilt Contest . . . . . . .Morgan Quality Products
    Group . . . . .Mettler® Imported by A&E®, Inc.
Handmade Quilts
    Handmade Quilts . . . . .Hoffman California Fabrics
Large Wall Quilts
    Appliqué . . . . .Fairfield Processing Corp.
    Pieced . . . . .Coats & Clark
    Mixed Techniques . . . . .Robert Kaufman Co., Inc.
Small Wall Quilts
    Traditional .FreeSpirit
    Non-traditional . . . . .Prym-Dritz Corporation
    Pictorial . . . . .Husqvarna Viking
    1st Entry in AQS Quilt Contest . . . . . . .YLI®
    Group . . . . .C&T Publishing
Miniature . . . . .Benartex, Inc.
Youth . . . .
Judges Recognition . . . . .Possibilities®
Viewer's Choice .American Quilter's Society
Fashion Show . . . . .American Quilter's Society, Hobbs Bonded Fibers
. . . . .Bernina® of America, Inc.
Sneak Preview . . . . .Ardco™ by Quiltsmith, Inc.
Teach America 2 Quilt...Again!® . . . . .Singer®
General Sponsorship . . . . .Baby Lock® USA, Elna USA, Hewlett Packard,
. . . . .Koala Cabinets, Nancy's Notions®
. . . . .Quilting Treasures™
MAQS Workshops . . . . .Flynn Quilt Frames, Olfa®, Pfaff® Sales & Marketing
MAQS Contest . . . . .Fairfield Processing Corp., Janome America, Inc.
. . . . .Clover Needlecraft, Inc.
MAQS School Block Challenge . . . . .Moda United Notions